Bearded Dragon Health

Understanding And Maintaining The Well-Being Of Your Bearded Dragon

Raymond Jack Tyler

Table of Contents

CHAPTER ONE

INTRODUCTION TO BEARDED DRAGON

The bearded dragon, experimentally known as Pogona, is a famous reptile pet because of its docile nature and manageable care prerequisites. Native to Australia, these lizards are named for the "beard" of spiky scales under their throat that they puff out when compromised or displaying dominance.

Bearded dragons come in various colors and patterns, with the most common being shades of brown, tan, and yellow. They regularly develop to around 12 to 24 creeps long, with males, for the most part, bigger and more vigorous than females.

One reason for their prominence as pets is their generally quiet temperament. They can turn out to be very agreeable with standard handling, making them reasonable allies for both beginners and experienced reptile attendants.

In terms of housing, an open enclosure with a lot of space for climbing, basking, and it is crucial for hiding spots. A substrate of reptile carpet or paper towels is frequently suggested for simple cleaning, although a few proprietors pick loose substrates like sand or reptile-safe soil.

Being omnivores, bearded dragons devour both plants and insects. A decent diet for a pet bearded dragon normally consists of mixed greens, vegetables, fruits, and live insects like crickets, mealworms, and dubia cockroaches. It's important to give them a variety of foods to guarantee they get legitimate nutrition.

Proper lighting and warming are essential for the health and prosperity of bearded dragons. They require an intensity slope inside their enclosure, with a basking spot arriving at temperatures around 95 to 110 degrees Fahrenheit (35 to 43 degrees Celsius) and cooler regions roughly between 24 and 29 degrees Celsius (75 to 85 degrees Fahrenheit). Furthermore, UVB lighting is important for the blend of vitamin D3, which is fundamental for calcium digestion and prevents metabolic bone disease.

Standard veterinary check-ups are prescribed to screen the health of pet bearded dragons and address any issues immediately. Common health concerns include respiratory infections, parasites, and metabolic bone disease.

Nonetheless, bearded dragons make entrancing and rewarding pets for reptile devotees. With legitimate care, consideration, and a reasonable climate, these delicate lizards can flourish in captivity for a long time.

UNDERSTANDING BEARDED DRAGON HEALTH

First off, diet is essential. Bearded dragons are omnivores, and that implies they eat both plants and insects. A decent diet consists of salad greens like kale, collard greens, and mustard greens, along with certain fruits like berries and melon. Insects like crickets, mealworms, and bugs are additionally important, particularly for more youthful dragons. Keep in mind that variety is vital to keeping them healthy.

Following up on temperature and lighting. Bearded dragons are cutthroat, so they need external intensity sources to direct their internal heat level. You'll require an intensity light or ceramic intensity producer to make a warm basking spot around 95–105°F (35–40°C). The remainder of the tank ought to be cooler, around 75–85°F (24–

29°C). Around evening time, you can allow it to drop a little, but never below 65°F (18°C). For lighting, an UVB bulb is fundamental. This assists them with delivering vitamin D3, which is essential for engrossing calcium.

Presently, onto housing. A proper enclosure is crucial for your bearded dragon's health. A 40-gallon tank is the base size for a grownup; however, greater is in every case better. Ensure the tank has a solid cover to forestall escapes and keep different pets out. Inside the tank, provide a variety of concealing spots and climbing surfaces. Natural materials like shakes and logs function admirably and assist with keeping them dynamic and stimulated.

Cleanliness is another important angle. Clean the tank consistently to forestall bacterial development and parasites. Spot clean every day by eliminating defecation and uneaten food. At regular intervals, do a profound clean, supplanting substrate, and sanitizing the tank and embellishments.

Finally, watch out for indications of disease. Common health issues in bearded dragons incorporate metabolic bone disease, respiratory infections, and parasites. Side effects to look for include lethargy, loss of appetite, expanding around the jaw, and abnormal excrement. In the event that you notice any of these signs, it's essential to consult a veterinarian who has practical experience with reptiles.

Keeping a healthy bearded dragon includes giving a fair diet, proper temperatures and lighting, a reasonable habitat, normal cleaning, and checking for indications of sickness. With legitimate care, your bearded dragon can carry on with a long and cheerful life.

CHAPTER TWO

BASIC ANATOMY AND PHYSIOLOGY

Anatomy:

1.   Skin and Scales: Bearded dragons have hard, layered skin that gives them assurance. Their scales are made of keratin, a similar material as our hair and nails.

2.   Head: The top of a bearded dragon is three-sided in shape, and they have a column of little spikes under their jawline, which is where they get their name from.

3.   Eyes and Ears: Bearded dragons have huge, round eyes that give them

great vision. They additionally have ear openings on the sides of their heads.

4.   Limbs and Tail: They have four legs with sharp hooks for climbing and digging. Their tail is long and can be utilized for balance and, in some cases, as a cautious weapon.

5.   Inner Organs: Like all creatures, bearded dragons show at least a bit of kindness, lungs, liver, and kidneys. These organs cooperate to keep the dragon alive and healthy.

Physiology:

1.   Digestive System: Bearded dragons are omnivores, meaning they eat both plants and insects. Their digestive system incorporates a stomach and

digestion tracts where food is separated and supplements are consumed.

2.   Respiratory System: They inhale through their noses, and the air goes down their windpipe into their lungs. Bearded dragons are ectothermic, and that implies they depend on outside sources to manage their internal heat level, including their respiratory rate.

3.   Circulatory System: Their heart siphons blood all through their body, conveying oxygen and supplements to their cells and eliminating side effects.

4.   Nervous System: Bearded dragons have a mind and a nervous system that permit them to detect their current circumstances, move, and respond to

stimuli. They likewise have an exceptional organ called a "third eye," which is a light-touchy structure on the highest point of their head that directs their circadian rhythms.

5. Reproductive System: Male bearded dragons have two hemipenes (reproductive organs), while females have a couple of ovaries. During mating season, males will display dominance and courtship behaviors to attract females.

6. Thermoregulation: As ectothermic creatures, bearded dragons depend on outer wellsprings of intensity to control their internal heat level. They luxuriate in the sun to warm up and look for shade or cooler regions to chill in.

A bearded dragon's anatomy comprises hard, layered skin, a three-sided head with little spikes, enormous eyes, and four legs with a long tail. Their physiology includes an omnivorous digestive system, a respiratory system for breathing, a circulatory system for blood dissemination, a nervous system for detecting and responding to their current circumstances, a reproductive system, and a thermoregulation system to manage internal heat levels.

COMMON HEALTH ISSUES
Bearded dragons are famous reptile pets known for their docile nature and remarkable appearance. Like all pets, they can encounter health issues. Here

are some common health issues to look out for:

1.   Metabolic Bone Disease (MBD): This is a common issue in bearded dragons because of the absence of legitimate UVB lighting and calcium in their diet. Signs incorporate delicate or weak bones, quakes, and trouble moving. To forestall MBD, ensure your dragon approaches an UVB light and a calcium-rich diet.

2.   Parasites: Internal and external parasites can influence bearded dragons. Symptoms include weight loss, diarrhea, and lethargy. Standard vet check-ups and waste tests can help identify and treat parasites.

3.   Respiratory Infections: Bearded dragons can foster respiratory infections because of lacking temperatures or moisture levels in their current circumstances. Side effects incorporate wheezing, release from the nose or mouth, and lethargy. Appropriate temperature and dampness control in their habitat are critical to preventing respiratory issues.

4.   Digestive Issues: Impaction is a common digestive issue in bearded dragons. It happens when they ingest substrates like sand, which can't be processed and impede their digestive organs. Indications of impaction include loss of appetite, bulging, and stoppage. Giving a legitimate substrate, for

example, reptile carpet or paper towels, and observing their diet can assist with preventing impaction.

5. Egg Restricting: Female bearded dragons can encounter egg restricting, where they can't lay their eggs. This can be dangerous if not treated promptly. Signs incorporate lethargy, loss of appetite, and an enlarged midsection. Assuming you suspect your female dragon is egg-bound, look for veterinary care right away.

6. Mouth Decay (Stomatitis): This bacterial contamination influences the mouth and gums of bearded dragons. Signs incorporate enlarged gums, an overabundance of spit, and a terrible stench from the mouth. Great

cleanliness and a fair diet can assist with preventing mouth decay.

7.	Dehydration: Bearded dragons can become dried out on the off chance that they don't approach new water or, on the other hand, assuming their current circumstances are excessively dry. Side effects incorporate indented eyes, badly crumpled skin, and lethargy. Guarantee your dragon has a shallow water dish and keeps up with legitimate moisture levels in their habitat.

8.	Skin Issues: Bearded dragons can foster skin issues like shedding and skin infections. Indications of skin issues include skin shed, redness, and injuries. Legitimate mugginess and cleanliness are fundamental for healthy skin.

9. Eye Issues: Eye infections and wounds can happen in bearded dragons. Side effects incorporate redness, enlarging, and release from the eyes. Routinely cleaning their eyes and maintaining a spotless climate can help prevent eye issues.

10. Obesity: Overfeeding and the absence of exercise can prompt obesity in bearded dragons. Signs incorporate exorbitant weight gain and trouble moving. A fair diet and giving chances to exercise can assist with preventing obesity.

Customary veterinary check-ups, a legitimate diet, and a very well-maintained habitat are fundamental for forestalling and dealing with these common health issues in bearded dragons. Assuming that you notice any indications of an ailment or abnormal behavior in your dragon, it's important to look for veterinary care immediately to guarantee their health and prosperity.

CHAPTER THREE

INDICATIONS OF A HEALTHY BEARDED DRAGON

A healthy bearded dragon is dynamic, alert, and has a decent appetite. Here are a few signs to search for to guarantee your beardie is healthy:

Physical Appearance:

1. Clear Eyes: A healthy bearded dragon ought to have clear, brilliant eyes. Shady or indented eyes can be an indication of disease or drying out.

2. Healthy Skin: The skin ought to be smooth and free of any bruises, injuries, or indications of shedding issues. Shedding is normal, yet it ought to occur

in complete pieces with practically no patches abandoned.

3.   Firm Body: The body ought to feel firm to the touch, not delicate or soft, which could demonstrate inside issues.

4.   Well-framed Stools: The droppings ought to be very well shaped and not excessively runny or discolored.

Behavioral Signs:

1.   Active and Alert: A healthy bearded dragon will be dynamic, investigating its current circumstances and taking caution with its environmental factors. It ought to be receptive to development and stimuli.

2.   Normal Rest Patterns: Bearded dragons are diurnal, meaning they are dynamic during the day and rest around evening time. They ought to have ordinary rest patterns and not be lazy during the day.

3.   Healthy Appetite: A decent appetite is an indication of a healthy bearded dragon. They ought to enthusiastically eat their food, which ought to incorporate a variety of insects, mixed greens, and infrequent fruits.

4.   Normal Temperament: While some beardies can be more docile than others, unexpected hostility, over-the-top stowing away, or other surprising behaviors can be indications of stress or disease.

Environmental Signs:

1.   Proper   Temperature: Bearded dragons require a warm basking spot of around 95–105°F (35–40°C) and a cooler side of the enclosure around 75–85°F   (24–29°C).   A   legitimate temperature slope is fundamental for their thermoregulation.

2. UVB Lighting: UVB light is fundamental for bearded dragons to utilize calcium and keep up with healthy bones. Ensure your beardie approaches UVB lighting for 10–12 hours per day.

3.   Clean Climate: A perfect and very well-maintained enclosure is essential for the health of your bearded dragon. Routinely perfect and sanitize the

enclosure to forestall bacterial development and parasites.

Indications of Disease:

It's additionally important to know about indications of sickness or distress in your bearded dragon:

1. Loss of Appetite: An unexpected lessening in appetite can be an indication of sickness or stress.

2. Lethargy: In the event that your bearded dragon is curiously idle or torpid, it very well may be an indication of basic health issues.

3. Weight Misfortune: Fast weight reduction or a perceptible lessening in weight can show health issues.

4.   Respiratory Issues: Wheezing, open-mouth breathing, or release from the nose or mouth can be indications of respiratory infections.

DIET AND NUTRITION

1.   Greens and Vegetables: Bearded dragons need a variety of new greens and vegetables every day. A few decent choices include:

A.   Collard greens

B.   Mustard greens

C.   Turnip greens

D.   Dandelion greens

E.   Endive

E.   Escarole

G.   Bell peppers

H.   Squash

I.   Carrots (with some restraint because of their high sugar content) Consistently wash veggies completely and cleave them into little, manageable pieces for your bearded dragon.

2.   Fruits: Fruits ought to be given less often than veggies since they contain more sugar. Appropriate fruits include:

A.   Apples (without seeds)

B.   Berries (strawberries, blueberries, and raspberries)

C.   Melon

D.   Mango

E.   Papaya

Feed fruits as an intermittent treat, not a staple piece of their diet.

3.   Protein: Bearded dragons need protein for development and energy. Great wellsprings of protein include:

A.   Insects: Crickets, mealworms, superworms, and dubia bugs

B.   Commercial Bearded Dragon Pellets: Search for superior-grade, reptile-explicit brands. Insects ought to be gut-loaded (take care of a nutritious diet) prior to being proposed to your bearded dragon. This guarantees they give the best nutrition.

4.   Calcium and Vitamin Enhancements: Calcium and vitamin supplements are significant for a

bearded dragon's bone health. Dust your beardie's food with a calcium supplement with D3 a few times each week and a multivitamin one time each week. This is particularly important for more youthful dragons and females that are laying eggs.

5. Water: Bearded dragons don't commonly drink from a water bowl like different pets. All things considered, they get the greatest part of their hydration from their food. Notwithstanding, it's as important as ever to give them a shallow dish of new, clean water for them to absorb. Some beardies will likewise drink from the dish.

6.   What to Stay away from:

A.   Poisonous Plants: A few plants are harmful to bearded dragons. Abstain from feeding them avocado, rhubarb, or anything from the nightshade family (tomatoes, potatoes, eggplant).

B.   Insects: Abstain from feeding wild-got insects, as they might transmit parasites or pesticides.

C.   Greasy Foods: Cut off greasy foods like mealworms, as they can cause obesity.

D.   Canned or Handled Foods: Stick to new or frozen foods for the best nutrition.

7. Feeding Schedule: Grown-up bearded dragons ought to be taken care of once per day, while adolescents might be taken care of 2-3 times each day. Change the sum in view of your dragon's appetite and activity level.

8. Gut-Loading Insects: Prior to feeding insects to your bearded dragon, gut-load them with nutritious greens and vegetables for 24–48 hours. This expands their nutritional incentive for your bearded dragon.

FEEDING SCHEDULE AND PORTIONS

Feeding Schedule:

Youthful Bearded Dragons (0–4 months old):

- Insects: Offer 2-3 times each day.

- Vegetables: Offer every day

- Fruit: Offer 1-2 times each week.

Adolescent Bearded Dragons (4–12 months old):

- Insects: Offer 1-2 times each day.

- Vegetables: Offer every day

- Fruit: Offer 1-2 times each week.

Grown-up Bearded Dragons (1 year and above):

- Insects: Offer 2-3 times each week.

- Vegetables: Offer every day

- Fruit: Offer 1-2 times each week.

Insect Portion Sizes:

Youthful Bearded Dragons:

• Feed 10–20 suitably measured insects for every feeding.

Adolescent Bearded Dragons:

• Feed 5–10 properly estimated insects for each feeding.

Grown-up Bearded Dragons:

• Feed 5–10 properly estimated insects 2-3 times each week.

Vegetable Portion Sizes:

All Ages:

• Offer a variety of cleaved vegetables, about the size of their heads, day to day.

Fruit Portion Sizes:

All Ages:

- Offer little bits of fruit, about the size of their head, 1-2 times each week.

Example Feeding Schedule:

Monday:

- Morning: 10–20 insects (crickets, mealworms, or dubia bugs)

- Afternoon: Chopped vegetables (collard greens, kale, and bell peppers)

- Evening: Chopped vegetables (squash, carrots) and a little piece of fruit (berries, mango)

Tuesday:

- Morning: Chopped vegetables (endive, dandelion greens)

- Afternoon: 5–10 insects (superworms, phoenix worms)

- Evening: Chopped vegetables (turnip greens, mustard greens)

Wednesday:

- Morning: 10–20 insects (dark soldier fly larvae, silkworms)

- Afternoon: Chopped vegetables (cucumber, zucchini)

- Evening: Chopped vegetables (green beans, peas) and a little piece of fruit (apple, pear)

Thursday:

- Morning: Chopped vegetables (cilantro, parsley)

- Afternoon: 5–10 insects (hornworms, waxworms)

- Evening: Chopped vegetables (butternut squash, pumpkin)

Friday:

- Morning: 10–20 insects (crickets, mealworms)

- Afternoon: Chopped vegetables (broccoli, cauliflower)

- Evening: Chopped vegetables (yam, beet greens) and a little piece of fruit (kiwi, papaya)

Saturday:

- Morning: Chopped vegetables (arugula, bok choy)

- Afternoon: 5–10 insects (dubia bugs, grasshoppers)

- Evening: Chopped vegetables (asparagus, radish) and a little piece of fruit (grapes, melon)

Sunday:

- Morning: Chopped vegetables (spinach, watercress)

- Afternoon: Chopped vegetables (green peas, bell peppers)

- Evening: Chopped vegetables (brussels sprouts, celery) and a little piece of fruit (banana, strawberry)

Important Tips:

1.   Variety is Vital: Offer a variety of insects and vegetables to guarantee a reasonable diet.

2.   Gut Loading Insects: Feed insects nutritious foods like fruits, vegetables, and business gut-load diets prior to offering them to your bearded dragon.

3.   Calcium and Vitamin Enhancements: Residue insects with a calcium and vitamin D3 supplement 2-3 times each week for adolescents and every seven days for adults.

4.   Fresh Water: Consistently give new, chlorine-free water in a shallow dish.

CHAPTER FOUR

SAFE AND HAZARDOUS FOODS

Bearded dragons are omnivorous reptiles that require a decent diet to remain healthy. While they can eat a variety of foods, some are safe and useful, while others can be perilous or even harmful to them.

Safe Foods:

1. Insects:

a. Crickets

b. Dubia insects

c. Mealworms (with some restraint)

d. Silkworms

e. Black fighter fly hatchlings

f.   Locusts

2.   Vegetables:

a.   Collard greens

b.   Mustard greens

c.   Turnip greens

d.   Kale (with some restraint)

e.   Squash

f.   Bell peppers

g.   Carrots (every so often)

3.   Fruits (with some restraint):

a.   Apples (without seeds)

b.   Bananas

c.   Berries (strawberries, blueberries, raspberries)

d. Mango

e. Papaya

4. Other foods:

a. Cooked eggs (mixed or bubbled)

b. Commercial bearded dragon pellets

c. Pinkie mice (for grown-up dragons, just as an incidental treat)

Hazardous Foods:

1. Insects:

a. Fireflies (contain poisons)

b. Boxelder bugs

c. Caterpillars (can be harmful)

d. Lightning bugs

2.   Vegetables:

a.   Iceberg lettuce (no nutritional worth and can cause looseness of the bowels)

b.   Spinach (contains oxalic corrosive, which can tie calcium)

c.   Rhubarb (contains oxalic corrosive)

d.   Avocado (harmful to numerous reptiles)

3.   Fruits:

a.   Citrus fruits (can be excessively acidic)

b.   Grapes and raisins (can be poisonous)

c.	Rhubarb (leaves are harmful)

## 4.	Other foods:

a.	Wild-got insects (risk of pesticide openness)

b.	Processed foods (chips, wafers, and so on.)

c.	Raw meat (can contain hurtful microscopic organisms)

d.	Dog or feline food (not nutritionally adjusted for bearded dragons)

Ways To Feed:

1.	Variety is Vital: Offer a variety of foods to guarantee a fair diet and forestall nutritional inadequacies.

2.	Gut Loading Insects: Feed insects a nutritious diet (like vegetables or business gut-loading food) prior to offering them to your bearded dragon.

3.	Supplements: Residue insects with calcium and vitamin D3 supplements a couple of times each week to forestall metabolic bone disease.

4.	Water: Give new, clean water day to day. A few bearded dragons like to drink from a shallow dish, which may be clouded to support drinking.

5.	Portion Control: Screen how much food you eat to forestall obesity and digestive issues.

Bearded dragons are native to the arid and semi-arid locales of Australia. To give them a healthy and agreeable habitat in captivity, reproducing their natural climate as intently as possible is fundamental. Here is a straightforward manual for setting up the ideal habitat for your bearded dragon.

Enclosure

The size of the enclosure is pivotal for the prosperity of your bearded dragon. For a grown-up bearded dragon, a 40-gallon tank is the suggested base size; however, greater is in every case better. A bigger enclosure, for example, a 75-gallon tank, will give your pet more space to investigate and exercise.

Substrate

The substrate is the material that lines the lower part of the enclosure. Reasonable substrates for bearded dragons include:

1.   Reptile carpet

2.   Ceramic tiles

3.   Paper towels

Try not to utilize loose substrates like sand or wood shavings, as these can be ingested by your bearded dragon and cause impaction.

Temperature

Bearded dragons are ectothermic, and that implies they depend on outer wellsprings of intensity to manage their internal heat level. You'll have to set up a temperature slope in the enclosure to allow your bearded dragon to really thermoregulate.

Basking Region:

1.   Temperature: 95-105°F (35-40°C)

2.   Utilize a basking bulb or ceramic intensity producer to make a warm basking place where your bearded dragon can raise its internal heat level.

Cool Side:

1.   Temperature: 75-85°F (24-29°C)

2.   Place the cool side of the enclosure away from the basking region to give an agreeable retreat to your bearded dragon.

UVB Lighting

Bearded dragons require UVB light to use calcium and keep up with healthy bones. Utilize an UVB bulb explicitly intended for reptiles and spot it over the basking region. Supplant the bulb each 6 a year to guarantee it stays powerful.

Concealing Spots and Decor

Give your bearded dragon concealing spots and stylistic layout to make the enclosure seriously enriching and animating.

1.   Rocks and branches for climbing

2.   Hide boxes or caverns for cover

Dampness and Water

Bearded dragons require a moderately low mugginess level of 30–40%. Give a shallow water dish to drink, yet guarantee it's not excessively profound to forestall suffocating.

Diet and Feeding

A decent diet is fundamental for the health of your bearded dragon. Offer a variety of new vegetables, for example, collard greens, mustard greens, and squash, as well as live insects like crickets, dubia bugs, and mealworms.

Cleaning and Upkeep

Standard cleaning is fundamental to keeping a healthy habitat for your bearded dragon.

1.   Spot clean the enclosure from day to day to eliminate dung and uneaten food.

2.   Profoundly clean the enclosure and replace the substrate twice a month.

CHAPTER FIVE

PREVENTATIVE CARE

1.   Proper Housing:

a.   Enclosure Size: Give an open enclosure. A 40-gallon tank is reasonable for a grown-up bearded dragon.

b.   Substrate: Utilize a substrate that is safe, simple, and spotless, for example, reptile carpet, paper towels, or ceramic tiles.

c.   Temperature Slope: Keep a temperature inclination in the enclosure. The basking region ought to be around 95–105°F (35–40°C), and the cooler side ought to be around 75–85°F (24–29°C).

d.   UVB Lighting: Give an UVB light to assist your bearded dragon with creating vitamin D3, which is fundamental for calcium retention and bone health.

2.   Proper Diet:

a.   Variety: Offer a variety of insects (crickets, mealworms, and cockroaches) and vegetables (collard greens, mustard greens, and squash) to guarantee a reasonable diet.

b.   Calcium and Vitamin Enhancements: Residue insects with calcium and vitamin supplements a couple of times each week to forestall metabolic bone disease.

c.   Water: Give new, clean water day to day. A few bearded dragons like to drink from a shallow dish, while others might like to be clouded.

3.   Regular Veterinary Check-ups:

a.   Annual Tests: Schedule yearly check-ups with a reptile veterinarian to screen your bearded dragon's health and identify any potential issues early.

b.   Fecal Tests: Routinely test your bearded dragon's defecation for parasites to immediately forestall and treat any pervasions.

4.   Observation and Communication:

a.   Monitor Behavior: Focus on your bearded dragon's behavior, appetite, and activity level. Any progression could show a health issue.

b. Handling: Handle your bearded dragon routinely to assist it with becoming familiar with human association and to check for any abnormalities like irregularities, knocks, or wounds.

5. Hygiene and Neatness:

a. Clean Enclosure: Consistently perfect and sanitize the enclosure to forestall the development of microbes and parasites.

b. Hand Washing: Consistently clean up when handling your bearded dragon or cleaning its enclosure to forestall the spread of disease.

6. Avoid Potential Hazards:

a. Toxic Plants: Eliminate any poisonous plants from the enclosure, as they can be unsafe whenever ingested.

b. Pesticides and Synthetic substances: Try not to utilize pesticides and unforgiving synthetic compounds around your bearded dragon, as they can be harmful.

7. Socialization and Enrichment:

a. Environmental Enrichment: Give environmental enrichment, like climbing branches and concealing spots, to energize natural behaviors and mental feelings.

b.   Socialization: Communicate with your bearded dragon day to day to assist with forestalling stress and to fabricate a security with your pet.

DENTAL CARE AND ORAL HEALTH

Dental care and oral health are important parts of by and large prosperity for bearded dragons. Legitimate care can forestall serious health issues and guarantee your pet's solace. This is the very thing you want to be aware of to keep your bearded dragon's teeth and mouth looking great.

Normal Dental Structure

Bearded dragons have a bunch of sharp, needle-like teeth intended for holding and tearing food. Not at all like people, they don't have molars for biting. All things considered, they utilize their teeth to get and separate their prey.

Indications of Dental Issues

It tends to be trying to detect dental issues in bearded dragons since they frequently hide indications of agony or uneasiness. Notwithstanding, a few signs could demonstrate a dental issue:

1.   Loss of Appetite: In the event that your dragon isn't eating to the surprise of no one, it could have dental issues.

2.   Slobbering   or   Unnecessary Salivation: This can be an indication of mouth torment.

3.   Enlarging or Discoloration: Check for any strange expanding or color changes in the gums or mouth.

4.   Awful Breath: Persevering terrible breath can demonstrate dental issues or infections.

Preventive Care

Diet

A proper diet is critical for dental health. Bearded dragons are omnivores and require a diet rich in calcium and vitamin D3 to keep up with healthy teeth and bones. Offer a variety of foods, for example,

1.   Insects: Crickets, mealworms, and cockroaches are incredible wellsprings of protein and calcium.

2.   Mixed Greens: Collard greens, mustard greens, and dandelion greens are high in calcium and different supplements.

3.   Commercial Diets: Top-notch business diets intended for bearded dragons can likewise be important for their diet.

Oral Cleanliness

Ordinary cleaning can assist with preventing plaque development and dental issues. This is the way to keep up with great oral cleanliness:

1.   Water Bowl: Give a shallow water bowl to your dragon to wash its mouth, which can help in eliminating food particles.

2.   Vet Check-ups: Normal veterinary check-ups can help distinguish and treat dental issues early.

3.   Stay away from Hard Foods: Try not to feed hard foods that can harm the teeth.

Treatment for Dental Issues

On the off chance that you suspect your bearded dragon has dental issues, counsel a veterinarian experienced in reptile care. Treatment choices might include:

1. Dental Cleaning: Proficient cleaning to eliminate plaque and tartar.

2. Extractions: In serious cases, damaged or tainted teeth might be extracted.

3. Medicine: Anti-microbials or painkillers might be recommended to treat infections or diminish torment.

COMMON PARASITES IN BEARDED DRAGONS

Be that as it may, similar to all creatures, they can be helpless to various parasites. Here are probably the most common parasites that can influence bearded dragons:

1. Internal Parasites:

a.   Coccidia: This is a solitary celled parasite that influences the digestive system. Side effects can include runs, lethargy, and a deficiency of appetite.

b.   Pinworms: These are little, white worms that can live in the digestive organs. Tainted dragons might give indications like weight reduction, looseness of the bowels, and general shortcoming.

c.   Tapeworms: These fragmented worms can likewise dwell in the digestion tracts. They could cause comparable side effects as pinworms, including weight reduction and gastrointestinal issues.

d.   Roundworms: These are one more kind of gastrointestinal parasite. Side effects can be like those brought about by pinworms and tapeworms.

2.   External Parasites:

a.   Mites: These small, ruddy, earthy colored parasites can be tracked down on the skin of the bearded dragon. They can cause tingling, skin aggravation, and, here and there, even pallor in extreme cases.

b.   Ticks: Ticks can connect themselves to a bearded dragon's skin and feed on its blood. This can prompt skin irritation and, in uncommon cases, the transmission of diseases.

c.   Fleas: While more uncommon in bearded dragons, bugs can likewise be an issue. They can cause tingling and skin irritation.

3.   Protozoan Parasites:

a.   Flagellates: These are tiny parasites that can cause gastrointestinal issues like loose bowels and weight reduction.

b.   Giardia: One more kind of protozoan parasite that influences the digestive system. Contaminated dragons might show side effects like the runs, regurgitating, and a deficiency of appetite.

4.   Prevention and Treatment:

a.	Regular Veterinary Check-ups: Normal check-ups with a reptile veterinarian can help recognize and treat parasites from the get-go.

b.	Quarantine New Dragons: On the off chance that you're acquainting another bearded dragon with your assortment, it's really smart to isolate them for half a month to screen for any indications of parasites.

c.	Clean Climate: Consistently perfect and clean your bearded dragon's enclosure to decrease the risk of parasite invasions.

d.	Proper Diet: A decent diet can assist with helping your bearded dragon's resistant system, making them less vulnerable to parasites.

5.   Symptoms to Look For:

a.   Changes in Appetite: A decline in appetite or refusal to eat.

b.   Weight Misfortune: Perceptible weight reduction regardless of an ordinary feeding schedule.

c.   Lethargy: Surprising sluggishness or absence of activity.

d.   Gastrointestinal Issues: Looseness of the bowels, regurgitating, or abnormal stool.

e.   Skin Aggravations: Redness, tingling, or apparent parasites on the skin.

CHAPTER SIX

IDENTIFYING STRESS FACTORS

Identifying stress factors in a bearded dragon is fundamental to guaranteeing its health and prosperity. These reptiles can end up being stressed because of various factors, and understanding these can help in providing a reasonable climate and care. Here are some common stress variables to pay special attention to:

1. Inadequate Enclosure Size: Bearded dragons require an extensive enclosure to move around freely. A confined space can stress them out and prompt various health issues. Guarantee the enclosure is something like 40 gallons for a grown-up bearded dragon.

2. Incorrect Temperature and Lighting: Bearded dragons are ectothermic, meaning they depend on outer intensity sources to control their internal heat level. Mistaken temperatures and insufficient UVB lighting can stress them and lead to health issues like metabolic bone disease. The basking spot ought to be around 95–105°F (35–40°C), with a cooler side around 75–85°F (24–29°C).

3. Improper Mugginess Levels: Bearded dragons require a moderately low dampness level of around 30–40%. High dampness can prompt respiratory infections and stress. Utilize a hygrometer to screen dampness levels in the enclosure.

4.   Poor Diet: A diet lacking in variety and fundamental supplements can stress a bearded dragon. They require a blend of insects (like crickets, bugs, and mealworms) and vegetables (for example, collard greens, mustard greens, and squash) for a reasonable diet. Mistaken supplementation can likewise prompt nutritional deficiencies.

5.   Lack of Hideouts: Bearded dragons need hideouts in their enclosures to withdraw and have a solid sense of reassurance. Without legitimate hideouts, they can feel uncovered and stressed.

6.   Handling and Communication: Overhandling or inaccurate handling methods can stress out a bearded

dragon. They need time to acclimate to their current circumstances and ought to be handled delicately and negligibly to stay away from stress.

7.	Environmental Changes: Unexpected changes in their current circumstances, such as moving to another area or adjusting their enclosure, can stress bearded dragons. They favor a steady and predictable climate.

8.	Presence of Hunters: Assuming there are different pets or people that act forcefully towards the bearded dragon, it can prompt stress. Guarantee a safe and quiet climate for the reptile.

9. Inadequate Cleaning and Cleanliness: Messy enclosures can prompt bacterial development and parasites, causing stress and health issues. Ordinary cleaning and keeping up with cleanliness in the enclosure are pivotal.

10. Illness and Health Issues: Any hidden health issues or diseases can cause stress in bearded dragons. Standard health check-ups and brief treatment of any health issues are fundamental.

Indications Of Stress In Bearded Dragons:

1. Obscured coloration

2. Hiding or excessive tunneling

3.   Loss of appetite

4.   Quick relaxing

5.   Forceful behavior

6.   Lethargy or diminished activity

7.   Excessive pacing or glass surfing

CREATING A STRESS-FREE ENVIRONMENT

Creating a stress-free environment for your bearded dragon is fundamental for its health and prosperity. These reptiles are delicate to their environmental factors, and stress can prompt a variety of health issues. Here are some basic moves to guarantee your bearded dragon has a good sense of security and is agreeable in its current circumstances.

1.   Legitimate Housing

First and foremost, your bearded dragon's enclosure ought to be roomy and exceptional. A 40-gallon tank is a decent beginning stage for a grown-up bearded dragon, yet bigger is in every case better. Guarantee the tank has appropriate ventilation and is made of glass or plastic to keep up with intensity and moistness.

2. Temperature and Lighting

Bearded dragons are ectothermic, meaning they depend on outside heat sources to control their internal heat level. Keep a temperature slope in the tank, with a hot basking spot of around 95–105°F (35–40°C) and a cooler side around 75–85°F (24–29°C). Utilize a great UVB bulb to give the essential UV beams to vitamin D union.

3.   Hideouts and Climbing Structures

Furnish your bearded dragon with a lot of concealing spots and climbing structures. This will permit them to withdraw and have a solid sense of safety when they need to. You can utilize rocks, branches, and reptile hides to establish a more naturalistic climate.

4.   Appropriate Diet and Hydration

A fair diet is urgent for your bearded dragon's health. Feed them a variety of insects, like crickets, mealworms, and dubia cockroaches, as well as new vegetables and fruits. Guarantee that new water is accessible consistently, either in a shallow dish or by clouding the enclosure.

5.   Regular Handling and Connection

Handling your bearded dragon routinely can assist them with turning out to be more acclimated to human association, lessening stress over the long haul. Be that as it may, consistently approach them delicately and stay away from unexpected developments to forestall frightening them.

6.   Limit Noise and Unsettling Disturbance

Bearded dragons are sensitive to boisterous noises and unexpected movements, which can stress them out. Place their enclosure in a calm region of your home, away from high-traffic regions and boisterous machines. Furthermore, abstain from tapping on the glass or making unexpected developments while connecting with them.

7.   Keep a Perfect Environment

A perfect environment is fundamental for your bearded dragon's health and prosperity. Spot clean the enclosure day to day, eliminating any uneaten food, defecation, or shed skin. A profound clean ought to be done week by week, replacing substrate and cleaning all surfaces with a reptile-safe sanitizer.

8.   Screen Health and Behavior

Watch out for your bearded dragon's health and behavior. Indications of stress or sickness can include loss of appetite, lethargy, hostility, and uncommon coloration. In the event that you notice any unsettling side effects, counsel a veterinarian with some expertise in reptiles.

CHAPTER SEVEN

BEHAVIORAL SIGNS OF STRESS

Bearded dragons, similar to all creatures, give indications of stress when they are awkward or feel compromised. Proprietors must perceive these behavioral markers to guarantee the prosperity of their pet.

1. Change in Color: A stressed bearded dragon might show more obscure colors or stress marks, which are dark crisscross patterns that show up on their midsection and here and there on their sides. These imprints can turn out to be more articulated when the dragon is stressed.

2. Aggressive Behavior: On the off chance that your bearded dragon is

puffing up its beard, opening its mouth wide, or displaying a cautious stance, it very well may be feeling compromised or stressed.

3. Loss of Appetite: An unexpected decline in eating or refusal to eat can be an indication of stress. Bearded dragons are regularly excited eaters, so any huge change in their appetite ought to be noted.

4. Restlessness: Inordinate pacing or going around the enclosure can demonstrate stress. They may likewise continually attempt to get away or hide.

5. Tail Jerking: Fast tail jerking can be an indication of nervousness or stress. Watch out for this behavior,

particularly during cooperation or while acquainting new components with their current circumstances.

6.   Glass Surfing: This is the point at which a bearded dragon over and over runs or scratches at the glass of its enclosure. It very well may be an indication of stress or a reaction to feeling restricted.

7.   Hiding: In the event that your bearded dragon is investing more energy stowing away than expected, it very well may be attempting to escape from a stressful circumstance.

8.   Increased Disturbance: Ceaseless scratching at the enclosure walls or

furniture, alongside mad development, can demonstrate stress.

9. Change in Basking Behavior: Bearded dragons require a warm basking spot to control their internal heat level. In the event that they are staying away from the basking region or investing less energy there, it very well may be an indication of stress.

10. Vocalizations: While not generally so common as different signs, a few bearded dragons might murmur or make different vocalizations when stressed.

It's important to remember that periodic stress can be normal, particularly during environmental changes or new introductions to their current circumstances. Nonetheless, constant or extreme stress can prompt health issues, so tending to the reason for the stress and making acclimations to the dragon's current circumstances or care routine is pivotal.

Assuming that you notice any of these signs, attempt to distinguish the reason for the stress and roll out important improvements. Guarantee that the enclosure is set up accurately with appropriate temperature angles, concealing spots, and substrate. Try not to handle your bearded dragon unnecessarily or in a manner that might cause uneasiness.

Routinely observing your bearded dragon's behavior and climate will help you distinguish and address potential stressors instantly, guaranteeing a cheerful and healthy pet. In the event that you're uncertain about any progress in behavior or have worries about your bearded dragon's health, talk with a veterinarian or reptile subject matter expert.

SKIN AND SHEDDING ISSUES

Like all pets, they can encounter health issues, and skin and shedding issues are common worries for bearded dragon proprietors. Understanding these issues and knowing how to address them is urgent for the prosperity of your pet.

Common Skin and Shedding Issues

1.   Incomplete Shedding (Dysecdysis): Bearded dragons shed their skin as they develop. Once in a while, the shedding system doesn't go without a hitch, prompting patches of old skin to stay adhered to the new skin. This can cause disturbance and uneasiness for your dragon.

2.   Dry Skin: Lacking dampness levels in the enclosure can prompt dry skin. Dry skin can become flaky and may prompt intricacies during shedding.

3.   Skin Infections: Bacterial or contagious infections can happen on the off chance that the skin is harmed or compromised. Indications of disease include redness, enlarging, and release.

4. Mites and Parasites: Outer parasites like vermin can cause skin disturbance and uneasiness. These minuscule irritations can be challenging to detect, yet they can prompt critical health issues if not treated quickly.

5. Burns: Inaccurate temperature slopes or direct openness to warm sources can cause burns on your bearded dragon's skin.

Tending to Skin and Shedding Issues

1. Proper Husbandry: Keep a reasonable habitat for your bearded dragon. This includes giving the right temperature inclinations and dampness levels. A basking spot with a

temperature of 95–105°F (35–40°C) and a cooler side around 75–85°F (24–29°C) is great. The stickiness ought to be associated with 30–40%.

2.   Regular Showers: Absorbing your bearded dragon tepid water can assist with mellowing the old skin and work with the shedding system. A shallow shower for 10–15 minutes a couple of times each week can be valuable.

3.   Gentle Handling: Try not to pull or pick at a stuck shed. In the event that the shed doesn't fall off effectively during a shower, it's ideal to let it be and allow it to fall off naturally.

4.   Skin Creams: For dry skin, you can apply a reptile-safe lotion or a couple of

drops of unadulterated aloe vera gel. Try to pick items explicitly figured out for reptiles.

5. Consult a Veterinarian: In the event that you suspect your bearded dragon has skin contamination, vermin, or consumption, counseling a reptile veterinarian is fundamental. They can give a legitimate finding and suggest suitable treatment, which might incorporate anti-microbials, antifungal drugs, or skin medicines.

Preventing Skin and Shedding Issues

1. Customary Check-ups: Routinely examine your bearded dragon for

indications of skin issues, parasites, or wounds.

2. Proper Nutrition: A proper diet is fundamental for general health and can uphold a healthy shedding process. Offer a variety of insects, mixed greens, and vegetables to guarantee your bearded dragon gets every one of the fundamental supplements.

3. Clean Climate: Consistently spotless and sanitize the enclosure to forestall bacterial and contagious development.

CHAPTER EIGHT

NORMAL SHEDDING PROCESS

Bearded dragons go through a shedding process to develop and supplant their old skin. Understanding the shedding system can assist proprietors with giving fitting care and guaranteeing the health and prosperity of their pets.

Shedding is a natural and fundamental cycle for bearded dragons, as it permits them to develop and supplant their old skin. As bearded dragons develop, their skin doesn't extend like mammalian skin does. All things being equal, they shed their skin in pieces or in one complete layer to accommodate their development. The shedding system is additionally important for eliminating any parasites or microorganisms that might be present on the old skin.

The shedding system ordinarily starts with the bearded dragon's skin seeming dull and grayish in color. This is an indication that the old skin is beginning to loosen and isolate from the new skin. As the shedding advances, the bearded dragon's skin might become flaky and begin to strip off in pieces. This can now and again make the bearded dragon seem peevish or anxious, as the shedding skin can be awkward or bothersome for them.

Proprietors really should give their bearded dragons legitimate care during the shedding system to assist with working with a smooth and effective shed. Here are a few hints to assist your bearded dragon through the shedding and handling:

1. Maintain Legitimate Stickiness: Bearded dragons require a specific degree of mugginess to aid in the shedding system. A stickiness level of around 30–40% is great for bearded dragons. You can keep up with moistness by clouding the enclosure with water or furnishing a muggy hide loaded up with soggy greenery.

2. Provide an Unpleasant Surface: Furnishing your bearded dragon with a harsh surface, for example, a piece of bark or a reptile carpet, can assist them with scouring against it to aid in the shedding system. This can assist with

loosening the old skin and make it simpler for the bearded dragon to shed.

3.   Offer Standard Showers: Giving your bearded dragon ordinary showers can assist with mellowing the old skin and make it simpler for them to shed. Utilize tepid water and permit your bearded dragon to splash for around 10–15 minutes. Tenderly rub their skin with your fingers to assist with eliminating the loosened skin.

4.   Avoid Handling: It is ideal to abstain from handling your bearded dragon exorbitantly during the shedding system, as this can cause extra stress and possibly upset the shedding system. Assuming that you want to handle your bearded dragon, do so tenderly and

abstain from pulling at the shedding skin.

5. Monitor for Difficulties: While shedding is a natural cycle, checking your bearded dragon for any indications of complications is important. This can incorporate held shed, where bits of the old skin don't fall off totally, or indications of skin contamination. On the off chance that you notice any issues, talk with a veterinarian about reptile care.

EMERGENCY CARE AND FIRST AID

Assuming that your bearded dragon is harmed or giving indications of distress, fast and appropriate emergency care is vital.

Survey What Is Happening

First, ensure you and the dragon are safe. Move toward the dragon gradually and tranquilly to try not to cause more stress. Search for clear indications of injury or sickness, such as dying, expanding, or having trouble relaxing.

Secure The Dragon

Handle the dragon delicately and safely. Utilize a delicate material or towel to get it, supporting its body and legs carefully to forestall further injury. Try not to hold it too firmly.

Check Breathing and Heartbeat

Listen and feel for breathing and a heartbeat. A bearded dragon's normal breathing rate is slow and ordinary. Place your ear carefully shrouded to tune in for breathing and feel for a heartbeat under its front legs.

Stop Bleeding

In the event that there's bleeding, apply delicate tension with a perfect material or dressing to the injury. Try not to utilize human prescriptions like hydrogen peroxide or liquor on the injury, as they can be destructive to the dragon.

Forestall Shock

Keep the dragon warm to forestall shock. Put it on a warm, delicate surface and cover it with a towel or cover. You can likewise utilize a warming cushion on a low setting; however, ensure it's not excessively hot.

Transport to a Vet

Looking for veterinary care at the earliest opportunity is important. Regardless of whether the dragon is, by all accounts, approved, it's ideal to have an expert assess and treat it. Call your neighborhood intriguing or reptile veterinarian to tell them you're coming.

First Aid For Common Issues

Burns

On the off chance that your bearded dragon has eaten, cool the region with cold water or a cool pack. Try not to apply ice directly to the drink. Look for veterinary care for legitimate treatment.

Dehydration

Indications of a lack of hydration include depressed eyes, lethargy, and a loss of appetite. Give the dragon new water and a shallow dish to drink from. A vet can likewise control liquids if necessary.

Ingestion Of Foreign Objects

On the off chance that you suspect your dragon has eaten something it shouldn't have, for example, a little toy or plant, contact a vet right away. Try not to endeavor to actuate heaving without veterinary direction.

Respiratory Issues

Signs incorporate wheezing, trouble breathing, and nasal release. Keep the dragon warm and look for veterinary care for legitimate conclusions and treatment.

Prevention

Routinely look at your dragon's enclosure for any dangers, such as sharp objects or harmful plants. Keep the enclosure clean and keep up with legitimate temperatures and stickiness levels to forestall health issues.

PHYSICAL EXERCISE AND ACTIVITY

Dealing with a bearded dragon incorporates feeding and housing as well as guaranteeing they get sufficient actual exercise and activity. This is indispensable for their general health, muscle advancement, and mental excitement.

Enclosure Arrangement

Begin with the right enclosure. An extensive terrarium with suitable substrate, climbing structures, and it is significant to relax spots. The size of the enclosure ought to be no less than 40 gallons for a grown-up bearded dragon.

Basking and UVB Lighting

Bearded dragons need UVB light to incorporate vitamin D3 and use calcium. Place an UVB light and a basking light toward one side of the enclosure. The basking spot ought to arrive at a temperature somewhere in the range of 95°F and 110°F (35°C to 43°C).

Day to day Activities

1.   Basking: Bearded dragons are sun-adoring reptiles. Permit them to lounge under the intensity of the light for 10–12 hours every day. This assists with processing as well as giving them the important UVB openness.

2.   Climbing: Incorporate branches, rocks, and other climbing structures in the enclosure. Bearded dragons appreciate climbing and investigating their current circumstances. This additionally helps in fostering their muscles.

3.	Roaming Outside the Enclosure: Allowing your bearded dragon to wander outside its enclosure is an effective method for exercise. Ensure the region is safe and secure. Oversee them near forestall mishaps or departures.

4.	Hunting and Searching: Spot live insects in the enclosure for your bearded dragon to chase and eat. This copies their natural hunting behavior and gives them a mental feeling.

Handling and Interaction

Normal handling and collaboration with your bearded dragon can likewise be a type of exercise. Tenderly holding them and allowing them to stroll around can energize development and socialization.

Exercise Caution

While it's important to empower active work, consistently guarantee the safety of your bearded dragon:

1. Stay away from Overexertion: Don't drive them to exercise unreasonably, particularly on the off chance that they are not accustomed to it.

2. Screen Temperature: Ensure the basking spot and the general temperature of the enclosure are inside the suggested range.

3. Oversee Open air Time: Consistently administer your bearded dragon when they are outside their

enclosure to forestall mishaps or wounds.

CHAPTER NINE

SIGNIFICANCE OF EXERCISE

Exercise is significant for the health and prosperity of a bearded dragon. Very much like people, these reptiles need actual work to remain fit, keep a healthy weight, and forestall different health issues. Here's the reason exercise is significant for your bearded dragon:

Muscle Strength And Adaptability Ordinary exercise helps in creating and keeping up major areas of strength for flexible and adaptable joints. Bearded dragons are normally dynamic animals in the wild, continually moving around to chase after food and investigate their current circumstances. In bondage, they need chances to climb, run, and investigate to keep their muscles and joints healthy.

Digestive Health

Exercise plays a fundamental role in advancing great processing. At the point when bearded dragons are dynamic, it animates their stomach related framework, assisting with preventing stoppage and other gastrointestinal issues. An inactive way of life can prompt stomach related issues, including impaction, which can be hazardous for these reptiles.

Mental Excitement

Bearded dragons are shrewd creatures that need mental strength to forestall weariness and stress. Normal exercise gives them the chance to investigate their environmental elements, examine new items, and take part in regular ways of behaving. This psychological excitement is fundamental for their general prosperity and satisfaction.

Weight Management

Very much like in people, stoutness can be a critical health issue for bearded dragons. Absence of exercise and overloading can prompt weight gain and related health issues, like greasy liver sickness and respiratory issues. Regular exercise assists them with consuming calories, maintaining a healthy weight, and remaining in a great state of being.

Prevention Of Metabolic Bone Illness (MBD)

Exercise is fundamental for forestalling metabolic bone sickness (MBD), a typical and possibly deadly condition in bearded dragons. Standard development and openness to regular daylight (or legitimate UVB lighting) animate vitamin D creation, which is essential for calcium ingestion and bone health. An absence of exercise and a lack of UVB openness can prompt a lack of calcium and the improvement of MBD.

Improved Immune System

Regular exercise can help the insusceptible arrangement of bearded dragons, making them more impervious to sickness and disease. Active work animates blood dissemination, assisting with conveying fundamental supplements and oxygen all through their bodies. A solid insusceptible framework is fundamental for forestalling diseases and guaranteeing a long and healthy life for your pet.

FINDING A REPTILE VETERINARIAN

1.   Ask for Recommendations

Start by asking for recommendations from other reptile proprietors, nearby pet stores, or raisers. They can give firsthand encounters and direct you to a vet with a decent standing for treating reptiles, especially bearded dragons.

1. Check Veterinary Association

Consult the association of Reptilian and amphibian Veterinarians (ARAV) or similar associations. They frequently have catalogs of guaranteed reptile veterinarians that you can look through by area.

1. Research Online

Search online for reptile veterinarians in your area. Search for audits and tributes from other reptile proprietors to check the nature of the care given by the veterinarian.

1. Call and Ask Questions

Once you have a rundown of expected veterinarians, call their workplaces to pose explicit inquiries about their involvement in bearded dragons and different reptiles. Ask about their schooling, preparation, and any particular gear or offices they have for treating reptiles.

1. Plan a Visit

Prior to settling on a last choice, plan a visit to the veterinarian's office to meet the staff and visit the office. This will provide you with a superior feeling of the tidiness and incredible skill of the center.

1. Consider the Costs

While cost ought not to be the main factor in your choice, it's essential to think about the expenses for tests, medicines, and any possible medical procedures. Try to get some information about installment choices, and in the event that they acknowledge pet protection.

1.   Assess the Veterinarian

During your visit, assess how the veterinarian cooperates with your bearded dragon. They ought to deal with your pet tenderly and unhesitatingly, exhibiting an intensive comprehension of reptile care.

1.   Emergency Services

See whether the veterinarian offers emergency services or on the other hand in the event that they can suggest a crisis center that works in reptile care.

1.   Trust Your Instincts

Ultimately, pay attention to your instincts. In the event that you feel great and positive about the veterinarian's capacity to really focus on your bearded dragon, it's possible a solid match.

1.   Follow-Up Care

Whenever you've picked a veterinarian, plan standard check-ups for your bearded dragon to expeditiously guarantee its health and address any possible issues.

THE END